To Valerie,
Reach Beyond!

Marjorie L. Kimbrough

~BEYOND~
Limitations

~BEYOND~
Limitations

Encouragement and
Inspiration for the Start of Your
Career

Marjorie L. Kimbrough

ABINGDON PRESS / Nashville

BEYOND LIMITATIONS

Copyright © 1993 by Abingdon Press

This book is printed on recycled, acid-free paper.

Library of Congress Cataloging-in-Publication Data

Kimbrough, Marjorie L., 19
    Beyond limitations : encouragement and inspiration for the start of your career / Marjorie L. Kimbrough.
    p.   cm.
    ISBN 0-687-03081-1 (hard : alk. paper)
    1. Young adults—Religious life. 2. Work—Religious aspects—Christianity. 3. Success—Religious aspects—Christianity. 4. Young adults—Psychology. 5. Work—Psychological aspects. 6. Success—Psychological aspects. I. Title.
BV4528.2.K55   1993
248.8'3—dc20
        92-47416
        CIP

93 94 95 96 97 98 99 00 01 02 — 10 9 8 7 6 5 4 3 2 1

MANUFACTURED IN THE UNITED STATES OF AMERICA

For my sons,
Walter and Wayne,
affectionately known as Mark and Marty,
who each have the power to reach beyond.

Contents

Introduction

Reaching Beyond

 story is told of a young boy who was drowning. Fortunately, the boy's father noticed his son's distress and threw him a rope in hopes of pulling him safely to shore. The son held on to the rope as his father tried to rescue him. Suddenly the son cried to his father, "The rope is breaking." Calmly the father cried back, "Reach beyond the break and hold on."

What a simple solution! What would happen in our lives if, when we are confronted with breaking points, with limitations, we would just reach beyond the break, beyond the limitation, and hold on? Wouldn't it be wonderful if we had that kind of strength?

There will be breaking points in all of our lives; and, yes, there will be limitations, but do we have the ability to reach beyond them? Do we have anything to hold on to? Do we even believe that there is anything on which to hold, anything beyond which we can reach?

Reaching beyond is an act of faith. We must have the vision to see beyond the breaks, beyond the limitations. We must believe that the rope beyond is strong enough to hold us, and we must believe that if we hold on, we will be rescued.

In the story above it is the boy's father who is giving the instructions. The boy trusts his father and believes that his father will save him. As I consider the implications of this story, I wonder whether or not we have the same faith in our heavenly Father. Do we trust our heavenly Father's will for our lives and believe that he will save us? After all, without faith in the one who holds the rope and in his good intentions for our lives, we will perish.

Let us explore some of the ways we have of reaching beyond.

Part One
Developing Self-esteem

Chapter 1

Building Self-esteem

he single most important factor in having the ability to reach beyond limitations is self-esteem! I believe this emphatically! What we think of ourselves influences all of our abilities. Anything can be a limitation if we do not believe in ourselves. It is impossible to reach beyond if we do not believe we can. What do you really think of your ability? The way you answer that question automatically influences your ability. If you believe you can, then you can. But how do you get to the place where you believe you can? How do you build your self-esteem?

An Early Start

The easiest way is to have someone help you. The best place to begin would have been at your birth. Try to think back to your early childhood. Did you hear things like, "Come on, try; I know you can do it. Take just one step for Mama. That's a good girl/boy! I knew you could do it. I'm so proud of you! I love you so much!"? Or did you hear things like, "I knew it! You can't do it! You'll never amount to anything. You can't help it; you're no good, just like your father! Don't even bother; you'll just fail. I try to love you but you make it so hard!"? Depending upon the kind of reinforcement you received, you formed an early self-evaluation. So, you currently either believe that you can master just about anything you tackle, or you have very little self-confidence and believe that you will probably fail at whatever you attempt. If this is true, then why aren't we all positive image builders? I don't know. It would be so helpful if we were.

We build self-esteem through positive reinforcement. The earlier in our lives that reinforcement begins, the more self-confident we become. Although it may be an out-dated cliché, I still firmly believe that "the hand that rocks the cradle rules the world." Whoever does the nurturing in the home is the one who controls self-perception. In our culture it is most often the mother who has this responsibility, but the father can certainly do it. What if both parents actively sought to build the child's self-esteem? Just imagine hearing from those who are most precious to you and upon whom you are totally dependent that you are special, talented, attractive, intelligent, loved, even invincible—wouldn't you believe it? Of course, you would! And you would be well on your way to building a positive self-image and unbeatable self-esteem.

This is not an easy task. It will take practice. Start right now. Identify someone who needs to build their self-esteem. Say aloud:

"Sally, you are special."

"John, you are so talented; I really admire you."

"Jean, you are so attractive. The Lord has really blessed you with beauty!"

"George, I really admire your intelligence and wit. You will succeed in whatever you do."

"Kim, you have a family that loves you and believes that you are invincible. What a blessing!"

Just handing out sincere compliments does not cost a thing, and it does so much for the self-esteem of the person receiving them. The more you think about praising and building others up, the more natural it will become. Practice!

As you nurture and care for the children (and adults) around you, remember that their self-esteem may very well depend on the way you speak to and encourage them. Let them know that

you believe in their ability and that they can overcome any obstacles. Reinforce positive experiences; praise accomplishments; encourage additional effort to overcome perceived failures; be
generous with compliments on appearance and
dress; and let all children know that they are
important and uniquely made by God and that
they are loved both by God and by you. Do this
often and unceasingly for as long as you live. The
benefits your actions will reap could change the
world.

Start now by identifying a child with whom
you are acquainted. This may be a child in your
own household or one you only see on occa-
sion, but think about that child. Say those
phrases I mentioned earlier to that child as
often as they are warranted, and help that one
child to build his or her self-esteem. Just think
how many children would believe in themselves if one other person did. So many children
have no one. You can be that person. Let the
child know that you are watching, that you are
willing to tangibly reward achievements, and
that you are generous with compliments
regarding success.

When I was growing up, my parents encouraged me to make all As in school; and because
they expressed the faith in me that I really could,
I did. It was as simple as that. My husband says
that no one encouraged him to try to get all As,
and he never did until we met in graduate school.

Then he started believing if I could do it, so could he. Well, he used his own experience to encourage the young students in our church to pledge in writing at the altar at the beginning of the school year to make either the honor roll or the pastor's roll. To make the honor roll, the student must make all As and Bs—no Cs. To make the pastor's roll, the student must make all As. Those making the honor roll are treated to a banquet at the church, and those making the pastor's roll are treated to dinner at the restaurant of their choice. One student who had never been so challenged before, pledged to make the pastor's roll. Knowing that his pastor expected him to live up to his pledge, the student succeeded and graduated at the top of his high school class. He was awarded a full scholarship to Duke University! His self-esteem is operating at full capacity. He believes in himself because his pastor did. It only takes one person who believes in one child!

Persons raised and nurtured in this environment will know that they can reach beyond limitations, that there is something to hold on to. They will know that there is strong rope beyond the break, and they will be sure that God is holding the rope. It has been said that we are what we eat, and when one is fed a constant diet of admiration, success, and self-confidence, then one feels admired and becomes successful and self-confident.

Although it is important—most important—

that parents consistently work with their children in building self-esteem, other adults, especially teachers, can certainly assist in this process. Marva Collins, the Chicago educator and founder of the Westside Preparatory School, tells the story of the development of self-esteem among her young pupils. The only word that the children are not allowed to use is *can't*, and they are indoctrinated with the belief that they are the smartest children in the world. A belief like that can truly change a child's worldview and self-perception. *Stop*

Because Westside Preparatory is such a unique example of what one visionary educator can accomplish, it is often the site of visitations by dignitaries. One day while President Bush was visiting, he was approached by a five-year-old student who asked, "Do you know who I am?" Of course the President did not and responded, "No." The child proceeded to inform him, "I am the smartest child in the world! When you grow up, don't you wish you could be just like me?" You see, the child understood his own importance and intelligence, but he had no conception of how important or intelligent the President was. Self-esteem, self-worth—how vital to growth and development!

A Later Beginning

But what of you who have missed the childhood and lifetime nurturing? You must start where you are with whomever you have, and if you have no one, then you will have to do it alone. Your job is tougher, but it is possible. You must look at yourself in the mirror and admire the wonderful human being that you see. This of course will make you want to become that wonderful human being. It will also inspire you to set goals for your future and to praise yourself on your ability to accomplish those goals.

You will need to become the parent or teacher who reinforces your possibilities, but you must be ever mindful of the fact that God is the parent who really believes in you—after all, you are created in God's own image. He has a unique plan for you. The prophet Jeremiah attributes these words to God:

> Before I formed you in the womb I knew you,
> and before you were born I consecrated you;
> I appointed you a prophet to the nations.
> (Jeremiah 1:5)

Surely if God had knowledge of and a plan for Jeremiah, he also has knowledge of and a plan for each of us. Seek to discover and fulfill that plan. What is it that God has especially planned for you to do? What is your unique mission? God has not assigned you a bigger task than you can handle, so get busy. Accomplish it!

God is your constant partner; so, in fact, you

are not alone. You have God, and God will never forsake you. Can you do it? Can you be your own nurturer? You can if you really want to! Tell yourself that you can do whatever you really want to do. Remember that God wants you to be your best possible person. You can be that person. Claim it!

You may need to develop a daily ritual that will assist you in the development of self-esteem. Let's try to work out a simple one.

---

1. As soon as you awaken in the morning, thank God for the day and for the opportunity to develop your self-confidence. Promise to do all you can to become that special person you were created to be.

2. Begin your day with meditation and Bible study. Use a study book that includes both a meditative passage and an accompanying scripture reading. Taking just a few minutes before you begin your daily activities will strengthen you and help you to focus on the good that surrounds your life.

3. Take the time to exercise your body. You need the energy that daily exercise provides, and you need the assurance that

---

you are maintaining the most attractive body that is practical for you. Looking and feeling better gives one greater self-confidence.

4. Plan well-balanced meals, and take the time to enjoy eating them. Try not to eat standing up or driving in the car. The time that we devote to our own nurture assures us that we are loved. Treat eating like a luxury, and you will enjoy it more.

5. Maintain a wardrobe that is well fitting and attractive on you. (Remember that you do not have to spend a lot of money to have an attractive wardrobe.) Nothing destroys self-confidence more than clothes that are not attractive and do not fit. You will be pleased with how you look, and others will compliment you, thus building your self-esteem.

6. Plan to do something for someone else each day. Doing for others gives us a sense of self-worth. It makes us seem essential, thus giving us a reason for being. This may be a small thing like reading the paper to someone, or preparing or buying a meal, or writing a letter, or calling on the telephone, or going to the store, or giving a hug. Just

give a little of yourself to others to let them know that you love them. Love has a way of multiplying. When you give it, there's more of it to give. You will need all the love you can give as you seek to build your self-confidence. Know that whatever you invest in this process is well worth the effort.

7. Plan to do something for yourself each day. Buy yourself a present, or take a nap, or watch a television program, or read a book, but do something just for you, something that nobody makes you do. Be reminded of the fact that you are a person worthy of love and that you love yourself.

These seven steps will help you to become your own nurturer, but remember that God is nurturing you through you. You are his agent in nurturing and loving you!

Nurturing Others

I know that it is hard to be a self-nurturer, and you may find it easier to become the adult nurturer of a friend, another adult who needs to build self-esteem. There is a hidden benefit in taking this approach, for once we begin to nurture others, they automatically reciprocate. It's like love, you have to give it to receive it. What a difference we would see in the world if people would become fellow nurturers rather than fellow competitors!

What if we tried to build one another up rather than tear one another down? What if we rejoiced in the successes of others rather than plotted their failures? Just think about it, would it really hurt you to praise others? To compliment them? To encourage them? To let them know that you believe in them and are praying for them? And wouldn't it help you to know that others were doing the same for you?

There is a fable of the devil and his many weapons. Listed among the many weapons are greed, pride, lust, jealousy, envy, and power. Although each of these weapons contributes to making us agents of the devil and not of God, there is one weapon that the devil always saves for last. It is his most powerful weapon—discouragement. When we discourage others, they lose their self-esteem and are defeated.

Let me share a personal example. When I was working very hard to find a publisher for my book, *Accept No Limitations*, a young woman approached me and said, "I don't mean to be funny or anything, but what makes you think that anyone would want to read about your life?" This young woman was really seeking to discourage me. She was not nurturing or helping in any way to build my self-confidence. She wanted me to accept failure, to be discouraged. She could not have known that I would turn her words around and use them to motivate me to work even harder to see my book in print. I said to myself, "I'll show her!" and I did. But isn't it sad that she could not have said to me, "Hang in there. I know you'll find a publisher soon, and I can't wait to read your book!" With those words she would have been a nurturer, a builder of self-esteem. Instead she acted as one of the devil's agents using his most lethal weapon, discouragement.

I wonder how many times we have acted as the devil's agents to discourage others. How many times have we missed the opportunity to be nurturers for God to encourage others in their struggles to believe in themselves?

As a college instructor returned exams to a group of biology majors, he announced, "The student who made the lowest score ought to select a new major." That student was devastated, discouraged, and lost all sense of worth and value. It would have been so much more helpful if the instructor had asked to see the student who had made the lowest score and sought to counsel with her and discover why she had performed so poorly. If that student had been encouraged, given hope, then she might have found it possible to reach beyond the limitations that the low score imposed. But the words of encouragement and the time for counsel would have required an investment on the part of the instructor. Obviously, the instructor was not willing to make that investment. It is much easier to discourage than it is to nurture. Once one is discouraged, he or she simply disappears, goes away, and does not have to be bothered with anymore. When this happens, you have succeeded in using the devil's most lethal weapon.

That college instructor had probably never heard of our seven steps of self-nurturing, but you have the ability to follow our seven steps of self-nurturing, and you can encourage others to do the same. Appoint yourself as the praise-giver when others tell you of their accomplishments. Be generous with compliments, encourage others in the tasks they undertake, let them know that you believe in their ability to succeed, and let them know that you are keeping them in your prayers. How wonderful it would be to know that others are praying for us! Remember that your nurturing of others also nurtures you.

We build self-esteem from the cradle and on through life. We contribute to the self-esteem of others in our daily contact. We must decide to be supportive of others in their feeling of self-worth. We must admit that it will not detract from us one bit if we encourage others. In fact our loving support of others will make us better human beings.

Envisioning Our Task

Building self-esteem requires vision. We must be able to envision several things:

1. We must visualize ourselves as beautiful, creative, intelligent, loved, admired, respected, and essential to others. We only see ourselves this way if someone constantly tells us that this is the way we really are or can be. That someone may even be ourselves. We, of course, are essential to our own selves, so we cannot do without this wonderful person that we are.

2. We must see the plan that God has for our lives. We believe that God has a plan for everyone, and he has a plan for us. We believe that we have the ability to discover what that plan is and how to implement it.

3. We must visualize children as instruments of God who are in need of our encouragement and support. We are joint partners with God in building their self-esteem.

4. We must see ourselves as growing and building our own self-esteem each time we encourage and show love to others. We

know that their success does not in any way detract from ours.

5. We must visualize God holding the rope that is breaking before us, and because he is the one at the other end of the rope, we see ourselves reaching beyond the break and all the limitations of our lives.

Chapter

Confronting the Limitation

One of the most difficult things to do is to confront issues head on. Most of us avoid confrontation at all costs, but we will never overcome issues or limitations until we learn to deal directly with them. We must not be afraid of confrontation, for it is merely an encounter—a gathering, a meeting of issues, opinions, or persons; and when there is confrontation, there can be reconciliation.

Which Limitations Are Limitations?

First let's deal with the limitation. Why do you consider it to be a limitation? Does it interfere with some goal or plan you had hoped to accomplish? Is it a real limitation or does it only appear to be? A limitation sets a boundary, a point beyond which we cannot go. Suppose that you have just graduated from college and are looking for your first job. You notice a job listing in the classified section of the Sunday newspaper and you are confident that you are qualified to do the job if hired. However, at the end of the job description you see these words *Previous experience required.* How can you get beyond this limitation? How can you acquire experience if no one will hire you without it? Although this lack of experience appears to be a limitation, is it really? Consider the following:

1. Is there anything you did in college for pay or gratis that might satisfy the experience requirement? For instance, if your area of expertise is accounting and you were involved in a work-study program in one of the student accounting offices or the college accounting department, you might be able to convince your prospective employer to consider your work-study as on-the-job experience.

2. Can any of your college courses, research projects, or volunteer activities qualify as experience? Women who have been home-makers often face this same situation, but many of them managed household or PTA

budgets, scheduled carpools, planned field trips, and acted as dietitians without financial compensation. These activities certainly qualify as experience. So, sit down and think about your real experience; it may qualify.

3. Would you consider an internship with a company for a few months or even a year to gain practical experience in your field? This may not seem to be financially feasible, but remember that you have made it through four or five years of college without much compensation, and one more year will not matter significantly. (As you grow older, the years pass so quickly that you hardly even notice one year!)

4. Is there a temporary agency with which you can work in order to gain experience? Temporary agencies do not pay very much but they do expose us to opportunities for experience in the world of work. Sometimes they even provide us with exposure to companies that offer us permanent, full-time positions.

Your lack of experience may not be a real limitation. You are a person of high self-esteem, and you have the ability to convince that prospective employer to give you the opportunity to demonstrate your ability. You have the power to reach beyond.

Another scenario occurs if we are employed by a corporation with a policy (written or understood) that women, minorities, or those who did not graduate from a certain school are never promoted above middle management. If we happen to fit one of these categories, then we have met a limitation. Is it a real limitation or does it just happen that up to the present time, this promotion policy has been in effect?

You are qualified. You have documented the unique contributions you have made to the corporation. You have also observed the contributions of the other employees, and you know that your contributions have resulted in bottom-line profits to the firm. You have statistics to support this. In other words, you have your facts together, and you think you are ready for confrontation. But are you?

Before you confront the powers that be, you must have a plan of action. What if your statistics are shot down? What if a fellow employee is truly better qualified and has made a more profitable contribution to the firm? What will you do? Are you ready to submit your resignation or will you humbly bow your head and retreat to your office—if you still have one? Have you looked around to see whether there are other employment opportunities available to you?

Never approach confrontation without a plan for retreat.

What will you say when the confrontational meeting occurs? How will you request it? Let's map it out *before* taking action.

---

1. Give prayerful meditation to your employment situation. Be sure that the limitation you face is real.

2. Prepare a brief but thorough description of the unique profit-producing contributions you have made to the corporation during your employment. Do not compare yourself to or even mention any other employee. You must be promoted on your merits alone and not on the failures of others.

3. Prepare a brief outline of the plans you have for the new job you would like. Be as detailed as possible. If the job to which you aspire does not have a title, give it one. List the person or position to which this job reports, and estimate the profit or savings your plans would yield during a specified period of time after you have assumed the position. Remember that you are a person of high self-esteem, and you know you can accomplish the plans you have proposed. Be

---

willing to allow your supervisor to challenge you to make your plan work! If you feel the new promotion merits a pay increase, have a ballpark salary figure in mind.

4. If your well thought out and detailed plan is rejected, you must be ready for confrontation. You must be prepared to ask why the plan is being rejected, and you need to be ready to document the fact that no minorities or other selected categories of employees have ever held the type of position you have outlined. You need to be willing to ask, "Why?"

5. Realizing that these questions may cause alienation, either you need to be prepared to continue in your present job in an even less favorable environment or you need to resign.

A Word of Caution

Confronting limitations can be costly, and that is why you need to consider your options carefully before deciding to proceed with the confrontation. Whether the limitation is job related or not, you will have to decide what to do once all the cards are on the table. Where do we go from here? If you decide to seek employment elsewhere, then the perceived limitation may have been a blessing in disguise. There may await greater opportunity for you that would never have been discovered had you remained where you were. Sometimes we want what is not best for us. We simply need to prepare as best we can for the situation we face and then trust God to make it all work together for good. Because we are persons of self-worth, we will not count any rejection as failure. It will only be viewed as a different and more challenging opportunity.

Limitations Involving Others

What if the limitation has to do with a personal relationship? Sometimes we feel limited by the relationships in which we are involved. If this is the case, then a different type of confrontation awaits us. We must seriously consider why we feel the relationship is limiting. Does it prevent us from full development as a person of worth, a beloved child of God? Does it prevent our pursuing the careers or voluntary involvement we desire? Does it hinder our relationships with others? Are we willing to withdraw from further development of the relationship? Are we willing to give the relationship up altogether? How important is the relationship to us? These are the questions that must be asked and answered before we are ready to pursue confrontation. I am assuming here a relationship *other than* marriage.

37

If you are ready, let us consider these steps:

1. Pray for the person who you feel is limiting you. Pray for an understanding of your relationship to each other.

2. Make a list of the good that you feel is nurtured by the relationship. What does it do for you? Then make a list of the detrimental features of the relationship. What does it do to you? Why and how does it limit you?

3. Describe how you would like the relationship to be. What would you like to get out of the relationship? What would you like to give to the relationship?

4. Consider prayerfully whether or not you believe it is possible for the relationship to be what you want it to be. If this is not possible, are you willing to dissolve the relationship or at least limit its further development?

5. Confront the person. Share your lists, your prayers, and your desires. Ask for a response. Be ready to dissolve the relationship if it is not possible to remove the limitations that are imposed.

Again, this action may hurt, but it may be the beginning of a more Christ-centered exchange with another one of God's children. Perhaps the other person was not aware of the limitations he or she was imposing. Perhaps he or she did not know that you have other wishes or desires. That is why communication is so important. Confrontation is well worth the effort, for the benefits can be so immense. If the relationship is dissolved, one must believe that it had no opportunity for further development. Thank God for your having discovered this and move on to new relationships.

Let's impose an additional aspect on this relationship. Suppose the person involved is someone with whom you must continue to have contact. Then you must realize that there will be no help from this source as you seek to reach your goals. This limitation will be there, and you will have to reach beyond and hold on.

Now suppose the limitation you face is imposed by a person, but you do not feel close enough or involved enough with him or her to identify your association as a relationship. Simply stated, there is a person in the way of your obtaining your goals. This may be someone who is competing with you for the same job or for the same person to be their husband or wife. This may even be someone who simply does not want you to obtain your goals. Remember that the devil's agents are always busy. Do you dare con-

front them? You should certainly consider it.
Weigh your options. Is there anything to be
gained? Will the confrontation merely encourage
someone to continue to harass you? Be aware
that some people just try to upset you to see how
you will react.

Maintaining Your Integrity

I remember a boss that I once had who would
insult women or minorities whenever he was
alone with a person from one of these groups. I
decided to ignore him whenever insults were
hurled my way. As the insults became more
vicious, I became more stone-faced and changed
the subject as quickly as possible. He finally
asked, "How can you not react to comments like
that?" I looked him in the eye and said, "I do not
react because I know you want me to!" I would
not dignify his comments with a reaction because
I knew he wanted to start an argument and eventually upset me. There are many people like that.
By ignoring him, I was really confronting him. I
was saying, "I know you want to upset me, but I
refuse to allow you to manipulate me. I am not a
puppet, and you cannot pull my strings!"
Confrontation may be direct or indirect. If you
are not interested in preserving the association,
you may simply choose to ignore the antagonist.
If you need to clear the air, you may need to confront the person and the situation head on. If
confrontation is your choice, prepare.

1. Document carefully citing place, date, and the instances in which you felt the limitations being imposed. Record specifically how you felt you were being limited. This will help you become aware of whether the limitation you felt was real or imagined. It will also equip you to respond without hesitation during the confrontation.

2. Ask the person why he or she responded in a certain way. Ask the person if he or she is aware of the way he or she made you feel and ask if there is a way those actions can be changed. Remember that whenever you ask questions like these, you must be prepared to listen to the answers. We often ask such questions but have already formulated the answers that we want or expect to hear in our minds. The result is that we do not hear the answer being given. Listen, hear the answer, and accept it in the spirit in which it is given. This may require your using all of the self-esteem you can muster. You may not like the answer, but you asked for it, and you are big enough, strong enough, and confident enough to accept it.

3. Consider your options. What will you do if the person claims ignorance to all you have documented? What if they feel there is

no need to change? One real danger is that you will have alerted them to the fact that they are limiting you, and you will be at a disadvantage in future dealings with them. You will have given them the upper hand. But do not despair. Knowing that they have the upper hand ought to make you more sensitive and alert to their actions in relation to you. Remember the admonition of our Lord, "Watch and pray, all of you, that you may not have to face temptation. Your spirit is willing, but human nature is weak" (Matthew 26:41 JBP).

4. How can you turn this situation around so that it benefits you? You might consider acknowledging the fact that you are aware of the effort to impose limitations, but you have the capacity to reach beyond. You will find a way to reach beyond every obstacle placed in your way. You will testify to the fact that you have in God an ally who never loses, and you intend to call on him day and night. A boldly witnessed faith in God is always frightening to those who seek to limit you.

Prayerful consideration of all of the above will so disarm your antagonist that he or she may just move on to less challenging conquests. You are able to do this because you have a high level of self-esteem, you know who you are, you know whose you are, and you can and will hold on.

Personal Limitations

Now suppose the limitation you feel involves some fact about you. You do not have the money you need to accomplish your goal; you are overweight; you do not have the education you need; you do not have the brains or talent. You are somehow limited by *you*. What do you do then? The confrontation you desperately need is with yourself. You must ask yourself some difficult questions and you must answer honestly.

---

1. How badly do you want to reach your goal?

2. Are you willing to invest the time and effort that may be required to raise the money or lose the weight or acquire the education?

3. Would you sacrifice things you enjoy to practice or study longer and harder to accomplish your goal?

4. Is your goal realistic, attainable within a specified time limit?

5. Do you believe you can do it?

---

6. Are you determined to do it?

7. Will you trust God to direct you?

Never let anything over which you have control limit you. You are a person of self-worth and high self-esteem. You can do anything you really want to. You can reach beyond.

Consider Willie Gary—one of eleven children from a South Florida migrant farm family—who really wanted to go to college but was limited by his financial condition. After completing high school and being turned down by two Florida colleges, Willie used what little money he had to travel by bus to Raleigh, North Carolina. There he tried for a walk-on football scholarship, but the team was complete and the coach advised him to go home.

Being out of money but full of self-esteem, self-confidence, and faith in God, Willie did not take the coach's advice. He stayed, sleeping in the dorm lobby, cleaning the locker room, and eating the leftovers that other students brought him. He was doing his best to reach beyond the break and hold on. Eventually a player was injured, and Willie made the team. He went on to graduate from college, became a successful lawyer, and has donated more than $10 million to his alma mater. He really wanted to reach his goal, and he did not let the limitation of his financial condition hinder him. You're just as good as Willie is. If he can do it, so can you! [1]

There is one additional possibility. The limitation you face may be completely out of your control. You have studied all of the circumstances, and you not only perceive it to be a real limitation, but you also believe that there is nothing you can do to change it. What are your options? Just remember that where your ability ends, God's begins. Turn it over to him. Let Jesus fix it for you. Trust him. You may not understand the limitation, but maybe it was put in your path to redirect you. Perhaps God is steering you in a more excellent way. Just what is it that God could be directing you to?

When I think about God's redirection of our lives, I think about my son, Walter. Walter had always wanted to be a veterinarian and he had entered vet school. Although he had been an honor student, he was on the verge of doing something he had never done before—fail. I talked with him and assured him that he had not all of a sudden become stupid. I told him that if vet school was not working, perhaps God was redirecting him. I asked if he was really sure that he still wanted to be a veterinarian; after all, that had simply been a childhood dream. He thought

1. Connie Green, "Former Migrant Farm Boy Repays Big Debt," *The Atlanta Constitution* (Tuesday, January 18, 1992), p. A3.

about it and decided that his interests had really shifted to higher education. He withdrew from vet school, earned a scholarship to obtain his master's degree in higher education, and completed his courses with a straight-A average. He is currently seeking his Ph.D. in higher education and someday hopes to be a college president. The limitations he faced were simply God's way of showing him a more excellent way. I am proud of him and I constantly tell him so. He is now confident that he has the ability to reach beyond.

I hope my son learned what we all must learn, and that is to be prayerful and open to God's will. As we face limitations over which we feel we have no control—and we all will—remember who is holding the rope. We are in our Father's hands. Reach beyond the limitation, go around it, go over it, or even under it; but hold on!

Chapter 3

Understanding Those
Who Seek to Limit

here exist in this world some people who just seem to want to limit everyone around them. They are never happy when others succeed; in fact, they are often very unhappy people. They eventually discover that seeking to limit others never proves to be a source of happiness; however, the absence of happiness in their own lives does not prevent them from wanting to dictate the successes and failures of others. They seem to find satisfaction by feeling in complete control of other people's lives. The best course of action when dealing with these limiting people might be avoidance, but no matter how desirable, avoidance might not be possible. Even though we would prefer never to come into contact with them, we may have to. Perhaps, then, the next best option would be, as we discussed in the previous chapter, to confront them. While confronting people like this may be a source of great pleasure, our confrontation will probably never change them; therefore, undoubtedly, the actual best possible course of action is simply to try to understand them.

Why Persons Limit Others

What is it that makes one person seek to limit another? Does the limiting person feel threatened by the success of another? Is the person so insecure, so lacking in self-confidence and self-esteem, that he or she feels that someone else's success will in some way limit his or her own success? Or could it be that the person just wants to be mean and deprive all except his or her close friends and family of any measure of satisfaction in life? What is it? It may very well be any or all of these things. And if any or all of these things are true, what does that say about the person who seeks to limit others? Consider the following possibilities:

> 1. The person who seeks to limit others might be in need of more love and attention. We already know that that person cannot be very secure or confident if he or she feels threatened by everyone. That person may be

living a life that is lonely and loveless, and he or she is crying out to us for love. Is it possible that we could spend more time with him or her? Could we listen to the person's problems and encourage her or him to share her or his joys? Could we do things for the person that demonstrate the fact that we recognize him or her as a person of worth and wish for him or her the best life has to offer? Carefully consider whether you are capable of responding in this way to a person that you perceive as trying to limit you. It takes one who has great self-esteem to do it, but you can.

2. The person who seeks to limit us may need to come to terms with his or her own lack of self-worth. This may mean that one of the most helpful things we can do in our relationship with them is to help them in this endeavor. (Our help would, of course, involve confrontation.) We learned about confrontation in the last chapter, and now we must consider whether or not we are prepared to put our theory into practice. Can you ask the person, "What do you really think of yourself? Why do you feel that you can only be successful if I am not successful? Don't you realize how valuable a person

you are?" If you can confront the person who seeks to limit with questions such as these, will you?

3. The person who seeks to limit may need us to assume the role of nurturer. Are we prepared for that? Can you be the nurturer, the builder of self-esteem, to that very person who seeks to limit you? Are you secure enough? Do you have the capacity to love even the least of these?

In our effort to understand those who seek to limit, let us consider each of these three possibilities. First, what can we do if the person is in need of more love and attention? We will have to remember the charge Jesus issued to Peter when he asked three times, "Simon, son of John, do you love me?" (John 21:15-17). When Simon Peter responded affirmatively all three times, Jesus charged him with the responsibility of feeding his sheep. Persons who seek to limit others are those sheep. We feed them by loving them; we become like Jesus, a good shepherd. You might be saying, "I don't even like this person, so how can I love him or her?" As a Christian you do not have to like what the person is doing or even has become, but you must love him or her as one of the sheep for whom Jesus died. When you view people in this way, it is much easier to love them.

Now that you are beginning to see this limiting person in a different light, consider the good qualities he or she has. Really stretch here. There must be some good. Remember the popular saying, "God didn't make no junk!" What is there about him or her that you can compliment and truly admire? It may be his or her educational achievements, family, job performance, professional or organizational attendance record, appearance, or any characteristic, attainment, or possession that you can authentically admire. Concentrate on this and begin your program of attention. Such a program might include doing the following:

1. Be generous but sincere with compliments. Give compliments frequently, but make sure that you really mean them. If there is nothing about which you can be complimentary, don't say anything. Being discovered as being insincere will do much more harm than good.

2. Seek out and listen to any advice the person may offer. Nothing helps to build another's confidence and self-esteem like being asked for advice or even an opinion. We always feel somewhat superior to another who values our experience. We can

learn from the experiences of others if we will listen with an open mind. Sometimes just hearing about the experiences of others changes the way we feel about that person and helps us to value them as children of God.

3. Help the person with projects he or she has undertaken, and in every way you can work with the person to achieve success. Whenever we are working on projects that are of particular interest to us, we welcome helping hands. By experiencing working with others, we discover who they are and they learn to appreciate us. It is so hard to limit one who helps us to achieve success.

4. When the person who has sought to limit achieves success, be genuine in expressing praise and happiness for him or her. Sincere appreciation for another's attainments is a great bridge builder, for a constant diet of love and attention is just too hard to ignore.

The Need for Patience

Even if you follow each of these suggestions carefully, don't expect to see the results of your efforts overnight. One who has lacked love and attention in life will not accept it readily or enthusiastically. It will take time, but while you are waiting, you are also learning more about the person and you are beginning to feel some sense of understanding and appreciation for who the person really is. You will probably be surprised by how getting to know and appreciate another really helps you to love and understand the person. There is some good in everyone. Giving the person a chance to demonstrate it is the crucial test that we all must pass if we are to progress beyond limitations. Keep in mind that as you attempt to show love and attention to those who seek to limit, you are feeding God's sheep.

In addition to showing that limiting person love and attention, you must also seek to discover whether or not he or she feels threatened and if so, by whom. You may be the person who poses the threat. Think about it seriously. Is there any reason you or your job, family, or circumstances pose a threat? Before you answer, carefully consider every aspect of your life. Answer each of the following questions:

---

1. How do you interact with this person?

2. What do you have that this person does not?

3. What do you have that he or she might want?

4. If you were in this person's shoes, would

> you feel threatened by you? Now remember
> that I said, "if you were in this person's
> shoes"; I don't want you to answer as you
> would but as he or she would.

If you feel that in any way the person could be
threatened by you, then it is easy for you to
understand why that person seeks to limit you.
That person is seeking to protect his or her own
best interests. This is a natural instinct, and we
must respect it.

Now you must decide what, if anything, you
want to do about it. Are you willing to give up
the job, downplay your family, or adjust your circumstances so that they appear less threatening?
Once you have to deal with personal reassess-
ment, deciding what is most important to you, it
is easier to understand others.

While you are in the frame of mind to walk in
the threatened person's shoes, go a step further
and assume his or her role. As the person who is
threatened by and resentful of you, how would
you deal with you? Consider the following:

> 1. What would you want you to do or not do?
>
> 2. Are you willing to do that? Why or why
> not?

Once you are standing in his or her shoes you may have a better understanding of that person's feelings. It takes real effort to empathize, but that is what you must do if you really want to understand those who seek to limit.

Are You a Threat?

If you are the one who is viewed as threatening, you may want to reassure the person who feels threatened that you are in no way seeking to limit his or her success. In like manner, you do not want to feel that he or she is trying or succeeding in limiting you. After all, you are extremely self-confident, and you know that the other person's success is completely independent of yours, and it is your hope that your feelings will be reciprocated. There is room for all to succeed. We, as Christians, have neither time nor energy to waste on *limiting* and not *loving* others. Jesus charged not only Peter, but all who love him to feed his sheep. In not even the widest stretch of the imagination could feeding involve limiting, but it takes no stretch at all for feeding to totally encompass loving. This message of following Jesus' edict to feed his sheep must be conveyed in a spirit of genuine love and appreciation, and it applies no matter who is viewed as the one who threatens. That person must be loved and understood. That person must be taught to believe in the gospel message conveyed in the Negro spiritual, "Plenty Good Room in My Father's Kingdom." Not threats and limitations, but love and attention are the first keys to understanding.

I shall never forget the first time I really began to understand the tremendous power of unconditional love and attention. As my son, Walter, was approaching his third birthday, my husband and I had noticed that his favorite things were cars and fried chicken drumsticks. So we decided to plan a birthday party centered around those two things. Our selecting this theme would show the attention we had paid to his likes as well as the love we had for him in wanting him to totally enjoy his first real birthday party. We found birthday party invitations that featured cars, and we decorated the room in which the party would be held with cars. In addition to the traditional birthday cake and ice cream, we served fried chicken drumsticks. When that little boy saw the decorations and the food, he stood in awe with the biggest smile we had ever seen on his face and said, "Is all this for me?" At that moment we knew that he understood the meaning of love and attention, and we experienced the joy only brought by giving both genuinely.

Toward Understanding

This illustration may very well have multiple implications. It may imply that we need practice in genuinely giving love and attention and the only way we can acquire that practice is by first extending it to those whom we find it easy to love—our parents, mates, children, friends, or simply those who do not seek to limit. Doing so will assure us that we are capable of giving love and attention.

This illustration also implies that love and attention are appreciated and are powerfully rewarding. Another implication is that feeding Jesus' sheep is worth the effort involved, and mutual understanding between the giver and the given is the end result. As we demonstrate our ability to show love and attention to those whom we already love, we become aware of our ability to also show love and attention to those who seek to limit and whom we must be big enough to learn to love. Our taking the first step toward understanding them by offering more love and attention is a sure reward.

The second step toward understanding those who seek to limit might be to help them come to terms with their lack of self-esteem and self-worth. This factor is usually active with those who seek to limit, for those who have a high level of self-esteem and self-worth have no need to seek to limit others. They are sure that there is "plenty good room." As I mentioned earlier, whenever we seek to help others come to terms with their own lack of self-esteem and self-worth, we are involved with confrontation. But before we confront the limiting person, we must confront ourselves. Ask yourself these questions:

1. Do I feel secure enough to raise questions with someone else about his or her security?

2. What if the person I approach turns the tables on me and says, "The only reason you feel that I am limiting you is because you are so insecure yourself"? How would I respond to that?

3. How do I approach a person in whom lack of self-esteem is obvious to me?

Each of these questions demonstrates the fact that you will have to prepare your case. You will have to approach with documented examples that not only have led you to perceive of them as limiting but also have demonstrated their lack of self-esteem. This will require both patience and keen skills of observation.

Let us consider a few examples. Suppose you have been asked to chair a committee, lead a retreat, or direct a project. The person who seeks to limit you approaches and advises you not to assume the task because you will surely fail. When you question this advice, you are told that the last person who assumed the task failed, and you are being set up to fail in the same way. Then you must ask if he or she has ever been asked to lead. The answer will probably be no, and you will know that he or she does not want you to succeed at anything he or she has not even had the opportunity to attempt. In his or her opinion, this would surely mean that you are more successful than that person is and will serve to lower her or his self-esteem even more. If the answer to the question is yes, then you will know that either that person failed and cannot bear to see you succeed or is afraid that your success will be even greater than hers or his. Each of these situations would serve to threaten those of low self-esteem. You confront your limiter in this situation by reassuring the person that whatever you do will in no way be a reflection on him or her. The other person's worth is not measured by your accomplishments or lack thereof.

Suppose you are offered a promotion or a marriage proposal. Your limiter advises you not to accept and proceeds to criticize the offer. You can be sure that in the limiter's mind the offer somehow elevates your status above his or hers. Consider this and then seek to affirm the person by letting him or her know that the offer is not a measure of either your own or anyone else's worth. Position, possessions, and relationships are not criteria for evaluation, for all are precious in his sight. Neither the promotion nor the marriage would change you or your opinion of either your own or the other person's worth.

What if you suspect you are being sabotaged? As far as you can tell, you are not being considered for a promotion, but someone seems intent upon helping you lose your job. Somehow the important reports on which you have been working overtime are misplaced and suddenly reappear credited to someone else.

Your first task is to discover who is limiting you by the acts of sabotage. This may require some detective work, but keep your eyes and ears open. See who hangs around your office and has access to your reports. Notice who is the new person getting credit for your work. Also notice who is friendly with that new person. Then deal directly with the person being credited. You may decide to catch him or her completely off guard by rewarding them. You may plan a counterattack by playing the same tricks on the person and then making him or her aware that you, too, can respond in kind. This, of course, is not the response that I would expect from a Christian, for you are dealing with one who already has a lack of self-esteem, and your counterattack will only serve to threaten the person further.

You might, however, plan the counterattack and make the person aware of the possibility of executing your plan. This would give you the opportunity to try to convince him or her that your losing your job will not in any way benefit him or her. What your limiter needs is understanding and nurturing, and this leads us to our third step.

In order to understand those who seek to limit, we may need to nurture them. We may have to do the same things for them that we might do for our children or our other loved ones. This means that we will heap praise on them, spend time with them, pray for them, let them know that we are proud of them and are expecting great things from them.

We are always willing to listen to their problems, share our own experiences, and take the time to find out about their loved ones. As we sincerely express this kind of interest, we will notice a change. It is just too hard to limit someone who constantly loves, rewards, and encourages you. There are too few people like that around; we cannot risk losing any of them.

Understanding those who seek to limit may require our showering them with love and attention, helping them to come to terms with their own sense of self-worth, and investing the effort in becoming their nurturer. Those who seek to limit are drowning; you can help them to hold on!

Part Two

Defining and Claiming Success

Chapter 4

Understanding Ourselves

ou may be wondering why I chose to discuss understanding ourselves after rather than before discussing understanding others. Well, it is easier to deal with the problems of others than it is to deal with our own. So, now that we have a better understanding of why others seek to limit us, we must come to terms with whether or not we might also be guilty of seeking to limit ourselves. There are certain questions that we must raise.

---

1. What is it that we really want in life?

2. What are we willing to do to achieve it? Is

> it within the realm of possibility? Can we do it?
>
> 3. What do we really know about ourselves? Is there anything that we know about ourselves that we might be willing to or capable of changing?

Your Definition of Success

Because I am not a psychologist, I am not attempting to discuss the intricacies of self-analysis, but I do want you to take a close look at your life and what you believe it would take to make you happy. In other words, what for you would constitute success? Once we understand our own definition of success, we begin to understand who we really are!

Let me begin with my definition of success, and then I want you to get a pencil and paper and write your definition. Writing down what you believe makes it more of a reality. The fact that you can put your definition of success into words means that you can visualize it, imagine it, see yourself accomplishing it. Begin now to think about it, carefully choose your words, and at the appropriate time write down your definition.

Success according to Marjorie Kimbrough is personal satisfaction with one's attainment in life. Do you agree? What attainment would afford you with a feeling of success? What attainment would make you happy? Are success and happiness equivalent?

Now, consider your own definition. What did you come up with? Do you meet the qualifications inherent in your definition? Does your definition imply achieving any goals? Do you see yourself achieving them? Can what you've described be applied to everyone or only to you? Are you limiting yourself because you are not willing to make the sacrifices necessary to achieve your goals?

Keep your definition close at hand while we discuss my definition a little further. If success is personal satisfaction with one's attainment in life, then it is extremely personal, and what one person considers success another might consider failure. Thus it is possible for both Barbara Bush, who chose to be a homemaker, and Hillary Clinton, who chose to be a lawyer, to consider themselves successful. Although each in her own way is personally satisfied with her chosen path, we know that the women of Wellesley College did not want Barbara Bush to be their 1990 commencement speaker because, in their estimation, her success depended on her husband's attainment, not her own. I am sure that these women would have accepted Hillary Clinton with open arms. But Barbara Bush did speak for that commencement, and here are some of the more notable quotes from that speech:

67

For several years you've had impressed upon you the importance to your career of dedication and hard work, and of course that's true. But as important as your obligations as a doctor, a lawyer, a business leader will be, you are a human being first and those human connections with spouses, with children, with friends are the most important investment you will ever make. . . . At the end of your life, you will never regret not having passed one more test, winning one more verdict, or not closing one more deal. You will regret time not spent with a husband, a child, a friend, or a parent.[1]

It seems obvious to me from these quotes that Barbara Bush is very sure of her definition of success, and of course she is successful. However, Hillary Clinton—who said that she could have stayed home and baked cookies and had teas but chose instead to become one of the most successful lawyers in Arkansas—is also sure of her definition of success, and it is the correct one for her. Success is intensely personal, and these women certainly represent two of its many faces. I doubt that any two people would agree on a definition of success as applied to their own individual life.

What about you? What career do you choose? Perhaps you are like me. I wanted it all. I wanted to be the Super Woman who had a career, family,

---

1. "Quotes from Wellesley," *The Atlanta Journal and the Atlanta Constitution* (Saturday, June 2, 1990), p. A11.

and was an old-fashioned, expert homemaker. Each of these three areas of my life have at some-time suffered or at least been part of a compromise, but then compromise is not all that bad. I have simply considered it to be part of the sacrifice involved in attaining my level of success.

A Closer Look

Let us refer again to my definition of success as we look at the three areas mentioned above. Personal satisfaction composes the first part of the definition. This means that I must be personally satisfied with my attainment in each area.

When I consider career, I think of a role outside the home. I do understand that some people may consider being a housewife or househusband a career; however, in my view a career implies working outside the home. I wanted a job for which I would be trained, compensated, and regarded as professional. If I had not attained that, I would not have considered myself successful.

I did attain that goal in more than one career. I worked as a data processing professional for twenty-eight years; I have worked as a college and seminary instructor for five years; and I have been a writer, speaker, and workshop and seminar leader for the past several years. Although I am personally satisfied with my attainments in my career life, I have discovered along the way that the measure of success that I feel with regard to my career has nothing to do with the financial compensation I have received. I have felt professionally successful as a teacher for one-third of the salary that I earned in the data processing industry. I have been rewarded with embraces, smiles, and tears as a speaker and felt much greater satisfaction than when I was generously compensated financially. My conception of a successful career had nothing to do with a certain amount of financial gain, for my criteria of personal satisfaction did not and does not include a specific dollar amount.

However, my criteria for personal career satisfaction did and does include professional respect, which I believe is related to professional appearance. I always wanted to "dress up" to go to work. I did not want to wear blue jeans and sneakers. I wanted to have that look of authority that is associated with the traditional "dress for success." The real impact of this became very real for me when I presented the Bible study for the World Congress on Evangelism in 1992.

In addition to having prepared my lectures very carefully, I also selected my clothes very carefully. I do realize that before you ever open your mouth to speak, your audience has already formed an opinion of you based on the way you are dressed. Your care in grooming and your taste in clothes say more about you than your words. My audience consisted of mostly white male preachers, teachers, and church workers. I am sure that most of my audience was somewhat shocked to see a black laywoman presenting the Bible study. She might have been asked to lead a workshop, for that would have been the inclusive thing to do, but the Bible study, no! Why that would definitely be reserved for a white male preacher.

After I had completed several lectures an attendee commented that I was very knowledgeable, articulate, and professionally dressed. He said that in light of those facts, it was a foregone conclusion that I would have been well accepted. Then he went on to say that he wondered how well accepted I would be if I wore blue jeans and sneakers to deliver the next lecture. I responded, "I don't wear blue jeans and sneakers!" His comment only reinforced my belief in the importance of appearance or presence. Dressing the way I did gave me the self-esteem and confidence I needed and, at the same time, conveyed to my audience a level of professionalism that could not be denied.

Second, in addition to a career I wanted a family. This means that I wanted to marry and have children. I would not have considered myself successful if I had had children without being married. Becoming a single mother did not and does not appeal to me. Even before I knew, from firsthand experience, what was involved in raising children, I would not have elected to do it alone. For those who are voluntarily considering single parenthood, I ask that you think about the great challenge of giving birth to and raising a child to responsible adulthood. It is the most difficult job there is. Accomplishing it alone only increases its level of difficulty. Not only do the children being raised need more than one adult to consult regarding their adjustment to the numerous stages of life, but adults also need a partner to share the advice and counsel being dispensed.

Because I believe that God is in control of my life, I would have adjusted if I had never married or had children; however, I would not have considered myself to have achieved success in this area. I would not have felt personally satisfied. But I never have had to deal with that dissatisfaction, for I did marry a wonderful husband who is a minister of the gospel of Jesus Christ, a caring Christian, and a staunch supporter of my varied careers. God also blessed me to give birth to two wonderful sons and to raise them to Christian adulthood, which, believe me, is the answer to a Christian mother's prayers. I consider myself successful in the area of family life for I have achieved personal satisfaction with my attainments.

Third, I wanted to be an expert, "old-fashioned" homemaker. This means that I wanted to keep my house clean, prepare home-cooked meals, make cakes and cookies from "scratch," wash and iron my husband's shirts, and occasionally make my own clothes. Cooking, sewing, and cleaning were those skills that I perceived all expert homemakers to have, and I would not have considered myself successful without them. But I am accomplished in each of these tasks, for I can cook, sew, and clean with the best of them.

I remember quite fondly the times that my children volunteered to donate cookies and cakes for school functions. They would proudly announce to their teachers that their mother made everything from "scratch." Of course I would respond to their requests and make the items only to discover that none of the children got any of them. Upon investigation I learned that some of the teachers had hidden and later eaten my home-baked goods claiming that the children did not know the difference between store bought and homemade. They did. I am quite satisfied with my attainments as a home-maker.

A Case Study

Before I ask you to think about your own definition of success, let me tell you about a friend of mine whose definition of success involved a career and maybe a husband but nothing more. We will call her Mary. Mary chose a career in the data processing industry. She had an excellent job working for a major computer company and was being promoted on a regular basis. She was certainly satisfied with her attainments and was, according to my definition, very successful. Mary was transferred to Philadelphia and continued to make regular progress toward her goal of management.

Mary met a very successful dentist, and they were married. His practice continued to grow, and they purchased a beautiful house in Philadelphia. Then her company did what many companies often do: they offered her a management position, but accepting it required relocation. Mary would have to move to New York. If she had been single as she had been prior to her transfer to Philadelphia, there would have been no problem. But she had a husband who had his own career, and the move would involve a family decision. Mary's husband was not interested in moving. He was satisfied with his office location, clientele, and professional affiliations. He saw himself as the family's primary wage earner and felt that his wife should turn down the promotion and wait for a similar offer in the Philadelphia area. But Mary felt that she needed to take the promotion when it was offered. She had no guarantee that a similar offer would ever again be available for her.

After much discussion the couple decided that Mary would take the promotion, rent an apartment, and commute to Philadelphia on weekends when possible. They also decided that they would not have children, for they could not decide with whom the children would live. Both

Mary and her husband felt that their careers came first, and children would be an added responsibility that neither of them was adequately equipped to handle.

What do you think? Were they successful? Do you agree with their definitions of success? Remember that theirs was a personal decision that they reached together. Whether or not it was the same decision we would have made is not important. They were satisfied with it; and, at the time they made it, it was the right decision for them. It is not a decision I would have made, for in similar situations, I have always chosen to let my husband's career dictate our living arrangements. Children were much too important to me and to my definition of success for me to have made a conscious decision not to include them in my life.

With regard to Mary, the decision to take the promotion was the best thing for her career because she has been extremely successful. She has attained all of her career goals. However, it was not the best decision for her marriage. The separation and commuting proved to be more than the marriage could sustain, and she and her husband were divorced. She has since remarried, is very happy, but has stayed with her decision not to have children. That, of course, was the best decision for her and for any children she might have had. Mary truly is a career woman.

75

Your Choices and Your Power

There are choices. Consider them carefully as you contemplate your own definition of success. What can you say about the areas or goals you defined? Suppose we consider the questions raised at the beginning of this chapter. What we really want in life ought be included in our definition of success. Look again at your definition. Does it include what you really want in life? Although my definition was very broad, I refined it to specific attainments for me. You may not consider me to be successful, but that does not matter, for with regard to my success, mine is the only opinion that matters. Remember that each definition is personal. We cannot and must not stand in judgment of others when it comes to defining success. That was the problem that the women of Wellesley College encountered when they objected to Barbara Bush as their commencement speaker. Success is an extremely personal experience.

If you should decide with me to try to have it all, time management is a must. Let me offer some tips:

---

1. Start with a list of the things you must do. Assess every job to be done, and divide it into bite-size tasks. Decide which of the

---

tasks you will complete today, and be disciplined enough to stick to your decision.

2. Set a time limit for the completion of each job on your list. Each day make a new list—either mentally or on paper. If a job stays on your list more than three days, remove it because you really do not want to do it. It is just not important enough to you, for if it were, it would have greater priority. So why fool yourself by continuing to pretend that you actually want to do it? It is also true that if you know you will have to remove it from your list, you may decide to give it greater priority and do it.

3. Learn to use your idle time. Read or answer correspondence while waiting in the doctor's office or in the beauty or barber shop.

4. Learn to do more than one thing at a time. Iron while watching television. Fold or sort clothes while visiting with friends. Practice using several appliances at once. You can cook and wash at the same time. You can use the oven and the electric fryer at the same time.

5. Organize. Have a place for everything in

your house or apartment and keep it there. Arrange your clothes according to color and season to eliminate the lost time spent looking for the ones you want to wear. Start with a double inventory of both the food staples and the office supplies you keep on hand. Then when you use the last of any item, put it on your shopping list and use your spare. Nothing wastes more time than having to stop in the middle of a task to go to the store. Plan your meals for a week, and let one trip to the grocery store suffice. Double recipes whenever possible. It does not take nearly as much time to make twice as much as it does to make it twice. Invest in freezer containers, and learn to eat leftovers.

6. Shake the lazy habit. The job before you is organized into bite-size tasks. Do it—regardless.

7. Don't procrastinate. You may as well get it over with. You really do not have to raise the level of procrastination to an art form.

8. Delegate. Assign the jobs you can to others in your household or on your staff. You really do not have to do everything yourself. But once you make an assignment, let it go. If you cannot forget it, do it yourself.

9. Take a break. Plan time to relax, read the paper, take a nap, watch television. You will be refreshed to continue with your daily tasks.

10. Plan time to exercise. This will give you energy, and will certainly improve your health.

11. Evaluate daily. Did you do what you wanted to? Why or why not? Refer to your daily list, and cross off the things that are of low priority.

12. Allow time for God. Spend time in prayer and praise. Pray for those who love you and for those who upset you. The time you spend in worship will strengthen you.

If you truly want to have it all, you must plan, organize, prioritize, rejoice, persist, and evaluate.

The next question I raised as we began this chapter is the critical one: What are you willing to do to achieve the success you desire? Would you sacrifice food, clothing, wealth, health, moral values? Would you risk your life? Would you risk the lives or careers of others? What about risking your reputation? How important are values and Christian principles as you seek to achieve a personal level of success? All of these questions are so important in the world of the twenty-first century.

The political scene in the United States in recent years has been plagued with questions of values. Those seeking election to various offices have expressed concern that many Americans have sacrificed values as they have sought success, that the homeless and the poor are without hope, that one group of citizens is being treated unfairly, that many of the wealthy seem to lack concern for humankind. Many political candidates want to achieve their own levels of success while acknowledging only those who could or might in some way make a meaningful contribution to their goals.

And so the burning issue for this decade seems to be change. The questions were and are: How can we as Americans get off the treadmill of moral decay and reinstate the values long since replaced by greed and wealth? How can we redefine success? How do we deal with politicians that vow to do anything necessary to be elected? Is success winning the election? If winning is all that matters then we are often willing to sacrifice everything to win. Moral values are not even a consideration.

Using the example of politics may be foreign to you, but substitute your idea of success, and you can see how easy it is to lose sight of everything else in an all-out effort to achieve your goal. Then be reminded of the fact that once you succeed you have only attained temporary fulfillment.

What are you willing to sacrifice for that promotion or that office or even for your child's achievement? Would sexual favors be out of the question? Consider this scenario. Your boss needs an escort for a company function and has invited you. You had planned to ask your wife (husband) or girlfriend (boyfriend), but your boss has made it clear that you are being considered for a position that is completely within her (his) power to grant. You have also noticed that your boss flirts and makes suggestive remarks whenever you two are alone. How important is the promotion? How well do you understand yourself?

What if you and your boss are of the same sex and your boss is seeking sexual favors? How important is the promotion? How sure are you of your own sexual preference? Are you open to experimentation or change? In the 1990s and with the rise of gay and lesbian rights, this situation may become more and more of a possibility. How well do you understand yourself?

Further consider the real-life situation of a mother who was so committed to her child's cheerleading aspirations that she hired someone to murder the mother of her child's leading competitor. The thought was that the competitor would be so distraught by the death that her own child would surely win the cheerleading spot.

Or what of the seventeen year old who tried to murder her lover's wife? How consumed were these women with achieving success? And how distorted was their idea of success? The question of moral values is real as we contemplate our concept of success. Just how far would we go? What would we be willing to do? We are the only ones who can answer these questions, and our answers are as different as we are.

Perhaps you are saying that you would never murder or attempt to murder anyone to achieve success, but you might be willing to cheat, lie, steal, or in some other way compromise your moral values. I know that the rationale is that everyone does it, but should you? What are you really willing to do to achieve the success you have defined?

Another question raised at the beginning of this chapter that needs to be discussed is, "Is the success you have defined within the realm of possibility?" Are you capable of achieving it? Sometimes we define for ourselves goals that are not achievable. We cannot even vividly imagine it, yet we want it. When we find ourselves in this situation, we need to reconsider our goals. If you cannot honestly see yourself achieving it, then it is not a viable goal.

If I had defined success as winning the gold medal in the Olympics in swimming, I would never have been successful. I barely passed the water safety test required for graduation from high school! I do not enjoy swimming; I am not willing to train daily; and I cannot visualize myself on the gold-medal platform listening to the National Anthem! In other words, this particular goal is not achievable for me.

Let us consider some basic facts as we define success in terms of attaining goals. If a goal is to be a valid one, it must be conceivable, believable, achievable, and measurable. Look again at your definition of success. Surely your goals are conceivable, for you have formulated them. You were able to think of them and start to visualize achieving them.

Next, your goals must be believable. Do you believe you can do it? You are the only one who can answer this question. Do you have what it takes? Are you willing to invest the required effort, make the necessary sacrifices, and keep trying no matter how many times you might fail?

If you are still answering yes to these questions, you are ready for the next step. Is your goal achievable; that is, can anybody do it? If it can be done, can you do it? It may be a waste of time to set goals that are impossible to attain. Carefully consider this. Then remember that you must be self-motivated and determined to achieve any and every goal you set.

The final element you must consider is this: Is your goal measurable? That simply means that you must place a time limit on it. If you simply say that someday you will be a manager, you have not set a goal. If you say that you will be a manager by January 1, 1998, you have set a goal. We can measure that, for on January 1, 1998, we will know whether or not you have accomplished your goal. At that point you have a true measure of your success.

By thoughtfully reviewing the possibility of your accomplishing your goals, you have an opportunity to discover what you really know about yourself. I really know that I am not a swimmer, so I know not to set goals that involve an accomplished swimmer. You know whether or not you are a strong leader, good speaker, or accomplished cook; therefore, your goals in the areas of your weaknesses should be modest. If you are hoping to improve in these areas, your goals might graduate in complexity. Begin with goals that are achievable so that you can realize a measure of success. Nothing motivates like success.

The last question raised at the beginning of this chapter was: Is there anything that we know about ourselves that we might be willing to or capable of changing? I ask this question in the context of helping us achieve those goals that we have set. Do we really know ourselves well enough to be willing to change? Is it possible to change? Only you can answer that question, for you have to want to change to even consider it. Unless we are forced at gun point, it is amazingly clear that we do for and to ourselves only what we want to do. Our success is in our hands; only we can accomplish it.

No matter how you define success, as Christians we can agree that success is being able to see Jesus and ask, "Are you satisfied with me?" and know that the answer will be, "Yes!" Christians are still striving to reach that goal, for they are constantly reaching beyond.

Chapter 5

Seeking a Supportive Community

nce you have decided on your definition of success and those goals that you would like to attain in life, you will need a supportive community. This simply means that you will need people, places, and things that will be there for you when disappointment and misfortune come your way. And, believe me, no matter who you are or where you live, both disappointment and misfortune will find you. One of the biggest mistakes you can make is to believe that you can do whatever it is that you really want to all alone. This thought or false belief should never even enter your mind. Why would you want to endure disappointment and misfortune alone? We all need somebody to help us, support us, and give us the encouragement to go on and to hold on. We all need to hear a real, tangible, flesh-and-blood person outside ourselves saying, "Reach beyond the break, and hold on!"

Being Open to Support

After having spent so much time talking about those who seek to limit, we need to spend some time on those who seek to support. There are, of course, those who assist us in building self-esteem, and we have defined earlier how they help and support us, but there is also a need to have those around us who just wish us well, who offer a smile and a hand, who are willing to be companions and partners whenever we need one. Those people may not know how to help us build our self-esteem, but they do know how to listen. They know how to tell us that they have faith in us, and they know how to pray with and for us. These are the people who form our supportive community, and we must seek to surround ourselves with them.

I remember a college student who was having difficulty paying her bills. She knew that her family had done all they could to assist her, and with other children to support, they could not help her any further. She did not even write to tell them of her financial need; she just bore her burden alone. After several weeks, she finally found a part-time job and was able to pay her bills. During the Christmas break, she told her parents of the hard time she had had, but she assured them that with her job she was able to pay her bills and was doing fine. Her mother asked why she had not told them of her difficulty. The student answered, "I didn't want you to worry or to sacrifice any more for me. I felt that I was old enough to work it out alone." Although her mother was proud of the young adult she saw emerging from the baby to whom she had given birth, she said, "You never work out anything alone when you have others who will pray for you. You need every prayer you can get!" The kind of support that student would have received by just knowing that her parents were praying for her would have made it easier for her to hold on until she found that job. The fervent prayers of the righteous do avail much.

A person who is simply willing to be a companion may provide the support you need. Sometimes the most meaningful function we can fulfill is to be there for someone. Consider the United States Olympic gold medalist, Gwen Torrence. Gwen always wanted to win a gold medal in track, but this did not happen while she was single and could devote full time to her training. After she married and had given birth to a son, many felt that her dream would never be realized. But she still wanted her gold medal. Although her husband had no Olympic aspirations, he volunteered to train with her, to be her companion on the track as she ran. He and their son became her supportive community. They were there for her, and in the 1992 Olympics she won not one, but two gold medals—and a silver one for good measure. I doubt that she could have done it without her family. Their support gave her the inspiration to hold on.

I remember hearing a minister tell the story of a young couple whose only child suffered a very tragic death. Their spunky two-year-old daughter was the light of their lives, and they had great and extensive plans for her future. But one day that child went into the bathroom and started eating toilet paper. She absorbed so much paper that the normal flow of blood and oxygen was interrupted, and she suffocated. The couple were devastated, and called their minister seeking his counsel and support. En route to the couple's home he wondered what he would say or how he could help them understand why this seemingly senseless, tragic death had occurred. Upon entering their home, he did not utter a word, he walked up to them, put his arms around both of them, and let them cry. When they had gained their composure, they both said, "Reverend, we feel so much better."

All the minister had done was be there, and being there was the most important thing he could have done. He became the companion with them in their suffering. He provided the arms of God that said, "I still love you. I am and will be with you. You will survive, for this, too, will pass." The minister did what God directed him to do, for he became that real, tangible, flesh-and-blood person who gave them that big, comforting hug that made them feel "so much better." I wonder if we who are not in the ordained ministry (and all who are) respond when someone needs us and God is calling us to be there.

The supportive community that we seek accepts us for who we are and as we are. We do not have to wear designer clothes, have perfect bodies, or know the right people. We are viewed and valued as lovable no matter what our material or physical circumstance. A young woman with whom I am acquainted has spent thousands of dollars on plastic surgery hoping to find a supportive community that will accept her for her physical beauty. She does not understand that that kind of acceptance will never be supportive. What will happen if the surgery needs to be repeated or the body sags even after being tucked? Who will love her when she is not quite so beautiful? She reminds me of the biblical character Martha of Bethany who was worried and troubled about many things, but had not chosen the good part which could not be taken away from her. Her sister Mary had. The supportive community that we seek will help us to choose the good part. It will help us to avoid laying up for ourselves treasures on earth where moths corrupt, for we shall have treasures in heaven.

Special Times of Support

The supportive community is not only with us as we seek to fulfill our goals and dreams, but that community is with us as we bear our sorrows. We do not always win the gold medal. Sometimes our beloved children die. We are not always successful. Our dreams do not always come true. We desperately need our supportive community during our disappointments and failures. Although it is wonderful to share our joys with those who offer us support, it is imperative that they be with us to share our sorrows. We just need someone to be there.

One parent who was trying to help her child understand the fact that we will all experience trouble and disappointment in life said constantly in her dealings with him, "You'll understand it better by and by." These words are a personalization of those found in Charles Albert Tindley's hymn. The verses of that hymn tell of the many trials that we face in life and the obstacles we must overcome before we receive our reward in heaven. The hymn's verses even cite the lack of basic necessities like food, shelter, and clothing often endured by those who seek to live according to the will of God. There is no guarantee that following his word will bring comfort and material success. But the refrain speaks of the promise of God that is guaranteed by the death and resurrection of Jesus. Its words are:

By and by, when the morning comes,
when the saints of God are gathered home,
we'll tell the story how we've overcome;
for we'll understand it better by and by. [1]

That parent knew that even if her child suffered, he would eventually understand and reap
the reward of living under the guidance and
direction of God. When the parent said her
words, "You'll understand it better by and by,"
the child did not understand what she meant. He
had not lived long enough, and he thought that
his mother was just repeating some religious jar-
gon that had no meaning for his life. But as the
child became a man, his understanding came
into focus. One day he called his mother and
said, "Mama, I'm in the 'by and by'!"

We all eventually get to the "by and by," and
when we do, we understand life better. When we
reach the "by and by," we have ourselves experienced the death of loved ones; we have suffered
with illness and pain; we have experienced or
have firsthand knowledge of others who have
been hungry and lacked shelter; we have seen the
devastation of earthquakes and tornadoes. When
we are further along the road of life and we, as
Charles Albert Tindley wrote, are able to "tell

---

1. Charles Albert Tindley, "We'll Understand It Better By
and By," *The United Methodist Hymnal* (Nashville: The
United Methodist Publishing House, 1989), no. 525; also in
Songs of Zion (Nashville: Abingdon Press, 1981), pp. 55-56.

the story how we've overcome," we will indeed
understand it better, for we will be in the "by
and by." How comforting it is to have with us
along life's journey others who also are in the
"by and by." They form our supportive community.

We especially need our supportive community
when we experience the death of a family member. It is surprising to discover how many of us
do not even know the first thing to do when
death occurs. Many of us have not bothered to
draw up a will, we do not own a cemetery plot,
and we do not leave funeral instructions. Faced
with a situation like this, a supportive community would seem like manna from heaven.
Someone will need to be with us as we identify
the body, select a casket, purchase a plot, or plan
a funeral. Someone will need to be there a week
or a month or even a year later, after we have
overcome the shock and the loss has become
real. Someone will need to assure us that life
goes on, and we must also. Consider now who
are those members of your supportive community?

Who could you call just to be there, to walk
with you silently in your time of need? Who
would still be around after everyone else had
left? How many times have we heard it said that
we all have lots of friends during our successes
and few during our failures? Cultivate the kinds
of genuine friendships that become supportive

communities. This, of course, means that we must be the kinds of friends who *are* supportive communities. It may require some creativity on our part to notice situations that seem to call us to supportive community.

For example, I live in a neighborhood of busy homeowners. We wave to one another, but never really spend time together visiting and discussing our daily lives. One day I noticed lots of cars outside my neighbor's house. The cars returned for several evenings, and then there was a funeral procession. Because I do not normally read the obituaries, I had not read that my neighbor's son had died. Armed with that information, I called another neighbor, and we discussed what both of our families could do to offer support. After everyone else had stopped coming by and there were no longer cars in the driveway, I decided to visit and express my condolences. I felt that the sudden loneliness that usually accompanies the death of a loved one might have surfaced, and my neighbor was probably sincerely in need of supportive community.

I took some home-baked goods and asked if there was anything I could do. I discovered that the mother felt as though she would never recover from the tragedy of her son's death. I remembered having read and even written some meditations that dealt with death and asked my neighbor if she would like to have a copy of them. She smiled with a joy I had not seen, for she seemed genuinely touched that someone would give her a gift that could live with her and daily help her address the emotional stress she was experiencing. I returned with the book and have attempted to keep in touch, for although she did not need a supportive community in happier days, she certainly needs one in her hour of sorrow. Although we will probably never be the type of neighbors who run in and out of each other's back door to borrow a cup of sugar, I hope that she now realizes that I can be a part of the supportive community committed to helping her reach beyond the break caused by the death of her son and hold on.

Being Supportive

It may not take an occurrence as drastic as death to make you aware of your need for a supportive community. I remember working in corporate America and experiencing a complete change in management. I was the supervisor of a small group of workers, and under the new management all but one member of my group was transferred to a different department. This meant that those of us who were being transferred would move to another building, leaving behind the one person who was not being transferred with the rest of us. We had become quite a family, and we all felt sorry for the one member who was being omitted. I spoke to her and assured her that we would not forget her. We promised to meet regularly for lunch and to sit together at corporate meetings. This promise did not seem like much to her or to me, but it was all I could offer at that moment. The act of comfort she really needed escaped me.

While we were packing, my younger son, Marty, came by my office with an exchange student from London who was visiting our family. Marty was exposing the student to American corporate life, but in the midst of this exposure, they stumbled upon a young woman in tears because she had been omitted from a group with which she had found supportive community.

Marty asked why the young woman was crying, and although he seemed satisfied with my response to his query, before we left the office Marty approached the young woman and gave her a big bear hug. When I asked him why he had done that, he said, "She looked like she needed a hug." The young woman admitted that she did indeed need that hug, and it helped her to find the strength to hold on amidst the changes that she did not welcome. Although it had never occurred to me or to any other member of my group to offer support by giving her a hug, I was proud of my son for being sensitive to her needs and becoming a part of her supportive community.

I am thinking now of the time that being a part of a supportive community simply meant to be willing to listen. There was a young man who was struggling with his sexual preference. He could not talk with his parents about his dilemma, for he felt they had greatly contributed to it. He approached me by saying that he needed to talk and he knew that I would be willing to listen. I was glad that he saw that willingness in me, and we met. I discovered that he harbored a hate for his father because he felt that his father had repeatedly raped his mother. His mother's screams had convinced him that men, not women, should be the source of his sexual release. He needed to come to terms with his feelings of guilt and hate. I listened, advised him to seek professional counseling, recommended some scriptures and books for reading, and prayed with him for strength and guidance assuring him that God loved and cared about him no matter how sinful he felt. I let him know that even in his distressed state, he was worthy of love. All I could really offer was a listening ear, but he needed one.

The Reverend Dr. Joseph Roberts, Jr., pastor of the historic Ebenezer Baptist Church where Dr. Martin Luther King, Jr. served as pastor in Atlanta, tells the story of a poor, hungry and ragged boy who was looking in the window of a restaurant. A patron in the restaurant noticed the boy, and invited him in to join him for dinner. Although the boy was embarrassed to be in so fine a place, his benefactor became his supportive community and made him feel at home. After they had dined, the two left the restaurant and the boy noticed a beautiful car parked across the street. Again the patron noticed the boy's look of wonder and offered the boy a ride. While they were in the car, the boy asked the man where he had gotten such a fine car. The man answered, "My brother bought it for me." In amazement the boy said, "You mean your brother bought this fine car just for you? I wish I could be a brother like that!" Being, not having, a brother like that, is what supportive community is all about. If you could be a brother like that, then you will have no difficulty in finding the supportive community you seek.

The fact that you are reading this book witnesses to your having experienced a supportive community. If no one had supported and nurtured you at birth, you would not have survived. You had to learn to eat, walk, and talk; you had to learn to respond to love and care; and you are probably still learning to give love and care. If you are a parent, then you have learned to be the supportive community to your child, and if you live long enough, you will again need a supportive community to provide for you. We may not want to grow old, but we certainly do not want to die. Growing old is the only alternative.

I think now of my friend Valerie who, along with her entire family, became a supportive community for her grandparents. We hear much about grandparents who are thrown away. Some have been taken away from home and deserted on the street; some have been deserted in nursing homes with no one to visit, listen to, or support them in their efforts to continue to live active and productive lives in spite of the onset of old age and ill health; and some with Alzheimer's disease have been the victims of mercy killings because no one had the time, patience, or interest to "hang in there" with them. Others without apparent infirmity have just died because they did not have the love and care necessary to sustain the desire to live. But Valerie's grandparents had a supportive community in her and her family.

Valerie expanded her home to include a beautiful apartment especially for them. She hired people to cook and clean for them when she could not, and her husband and children worked with her to provide the loving care that is certain to help her grandparents live much longer and more fruitful lives. What a beautiful witness to her children! They are gaining firsthand knowledge of the needs of aging. Not only will they be prepared to be caregivers when their parents are the ages of their great-grandparents, but they are also experiencing love in action. Look within for your supportive community. You may be surprised to find it right where you are.

These examples help illustrate the fact that we truly reap what we sow. In order to find the supportive community that we seek, we must become a supportive community. If we want to have friends, we must be a friend. This is so simple, yet everyday I talk with people who are distressed because they have no friends, but I soon discover that they have never been a friend. I am reminded of the words of Kahlil Gibran:

> Your friend is your needs answered,
> He is your field which you sow with love
> and reap with thanksgiving,
> And he is your board and your fireside.
> For you come to him with your hunger,
> and you seek him for peace.[2]

Your friend, your supportive community, do indeed answer your needs, but you have sown that seed, that field, with love. Friends are not friends in a vacuum; they are friends in response to love. You invest the love and you reap the benefit of friendship. Seeking a supportive community will cost you an investment of love.

Jesus told us about the supportive community. He told us to be the servant of all, to wash one another's feet, to forgive one another not one time but seventy times seven times, and to lay down our lives for our friends. These instructions clarify the investment we are expected to make.

---

2. Kahlil Gibran, *The Prophet* (New York: Alfred A. Knopf, 1965), p. 58.

101

Hierophanies

At the beginning of this chapter I mentioned finding our supportive community not only in people but also in places and things. Hierophanies are defined as ways in which the sacred is manifested, and they can assume the form of people, places, or things.[3] A supportive community is certainly a hierophany, for the sacred is manifested through it. Whenever something or someone lifts you up and encourages you, you are experiencing the manifestation of the sacred. This further means that supportive communities can be places. You may experience your supportive community at a lake side, in a church, in a park, or on a beach. Just going to that special place, hierophany, of yours provides the supportive community that you need. Find your own personal, special place. Visit it often. Let its blessing surround you and give you peace.

I find almost any place where there is a clear, beautiful body of water to be a hierophany. I remember the words of Jesus as he spoke to the woman at the well promising life-giving water. He told her that those who drank of the water that he gave would never thirst again, and I know that when I seek my special place, I want the thirst in my soul to go away. Just being there by

---

3. *Eerdmans' Handbook to the World's Religions* (Grand Rapids: Wm. B. Eerdmans, 1982), p. 18.

that water, I can see Jesus and realize there is eternal life. Think about your special place, your hierophany.

Your hierophany, your supportive community, may be a thing. It may be a cross, a stone, a picture, or an article of clothing. I remember a woman who spoke of the jacket her husband had worn before he left to fight in the Gulf War. Wearing the jacket or even just touching the jacket seemed to bring her husband to her. She could feel and smell his presence through the thing, and it became for her a source of support.

Is there a loved one who is manifested to you through some thing that they gave you or once owned? If so, then holding or clutching that thing can be your supportive community. Pictures can, of course, evoke memories and make people more real to you, and through them you can experience support. You see, if you do not presently have the friends who will become your supportive community, you may have some places and things that can fill in for the time being. However, I hope that you are thinking about being a friend so that your time without friends and only with things will be brief.

There is one additional source of supportive community that I want to explore. It involves hobbies and organizations. You may have interests in books, music, stamps, cooking, auto repair, flying, or whatever. Cultivate that interest or hobby into a source of supportive community. I find reading and writing a source of support. I can relate to the authors and characters of books, and either forget my own source of distress or share in their joy. I can be encouraged by others both real and fictional who have held on and know that I can do it, too. I can be uplifted by passages of scripture or religious testimony and know that God is still in the blessing business and he has and will bless me.

Your interests and hobbies can lead you to organizations where you will find people with similar interests, and they will become your supportive community as you become theirs. I would summarize our seeking a supportive community as:

1. Find, attend, and join a church that speaks to and satisfies your spiritual needs. Attend your church regularly and get to know its members by becoming actively involved.

2. Go to the meetings of special interest groups. Join the clubs composed of people with interests that are similar to yours. Get involved in their projects, and volunteer to assume some leadership responsibilities.

3. Be sensitive to and provide support to those who need it no matter where you find

> them. They may be your neighbors or your
> co-workers or even members of your own
> family. Remember that the most important
> thing you can do is be there.

These three steps will help us find the supportive community that we all seek. Our supportive community, our hierophanies, are indeed people, places, and things, but the greatest of these are people.

Part Three

Finding Sustenance

Chapter 6

Committing to God

*T*hroughout this book I have sought to describe how we can reach beyond the limitations that confront us. First, we must have the desire to reach beyond. Some of us simply do not want to make the effort to overcome our limitations; we would rather commiserate with ourselves and others about the unfair limitations that have been placed upon us. We constantly review our real and imagined limitations and decide that the investment of self required to overcome them is more than we can bear.

Acknowledging Our Need

Oh, how unfortunate it is for us whenever we consciously decide not even to try to reach beyond our limitations! I say this because I have found it to be true that we all basically do whatever it is that we really want to do. Doing something, doing anything, just getting involved would require that we become proactive, and for many of us it is so much easier to convince ourselves that we are satisfied where and with what we are. "Let someone else do it; I'm too old, too weak, too frail." Of course, if we assume this attitude, we have not digested the second step, which was building self-esteem. One who has self-esteem and an abundance of confidence is determined to reach beyond, for they know they can overcome all limitations.

That person is ready for the third step which is confronting the limitation head on. The fourth and fifth steps involve understanding not only those who seek to limit us but also ourselves. The sixth step is seeking (and becoming a part of) a supportive community, and the final step is committing to the Father.

As we begin our discussion of this final step, let me acknowledge my use of traditional language. If you see God as Mother, then feel free to substitute Mother where I use Father. I just happen to view God as Father because Jesus referred to him as Father, but my Father concept is inclusive of maternal attributes.

We must commit to the Father because he is the source of our sustenance. He is the one who keeps us going, reaching beyond, for he is holding the rope and we know that he will not let go. When that rope is breaking, he is the one telling us to reach beyond the break and hold on! He is our support, the little voice within us that keeps telling us that we can do and be anything we want to. If you never hear that voice, then your need for commitment is urgent. When others meet us with skepticism and seek to limit us, God is there. When we have inklings of doubt and despair, God is there. When we are attacked verbally, psychologically, and even physically, God is there. As the gospel song says:

> He promised to keep me, never to leave me.
> He'll never, ever come short of His word.[1]

God is our sustenance, and to connect with that source of sustenance, we must commit to him! There is no other way to do it!

What does it really mean to commit? Webster's dictionary defines *commit* as "to give in trust, to bind, to pledge." In connection with the heavenly Father, when we commit ourselves, we have given our lives in trust to him. This means that we are dependent on him for our survival. We will love and adore him, praise and worship him, confess our sins to him, ask him for forgiveness, and count on him for all our blessings. We believe with Solomon:

---

1. Robert Fryson, "God Is" (Washington, D.C.: Bob Jay Publishing Co., 1976).

> Trust in the LORD with all your heart,
>   and do not rely on your own insight.
> In all your ways acknowledge him,
>   and he will make straight your paths.
>   (Proverbs 3:5-6)

We are bound to him in such a way that we cannot possibly escape. Our connection is just that strong, and because of our pledge to him, we do not want to escape. We have literally pledged our allegiance to him for life.

We cannot expect anyone else, not mother, father, sister, brother, husband, or friend to be to us what God can be. They are all human; God is Spirit, and as Spirit, God can be with us all the time, everywhere. Only God can honor our commitment, for only God never leaves us. God is! God promised never to leave us, and he alone will not. Others may not want to leave us, but they are not in control of their lives. Life in all of its circumstances and perplexities takes control away from human beings. Yet we commit to them. If we are willing to commit to those who are not in control, should we not be willing to commit to God who is in control? And if we are, how do we do it?

Learning About This Commitment

If commitment does indeed mean to give in trust, then we must give ourselves in trust to God. Neither you nor I would give ourselves in

112

trust to anything or anyone that we did not know anything about. Why then do so many of us talk about committing to a God about whom we know nothing?

So many young people come to me asking me to tell them what we as Christians believe. They are often confronted by followers of other faiths who challenge their beliefs. The simple truth is that many young "Christians" have not yet earned the title. They are not even vaguely acquainted with the Bible; they do not know the history of the faith; they do not know the differences between Christians and Jews or between Christians and Muslims; they are not sure of the meaning of the creeds they repeat in church whenever they happen to attend. And the real tragedy is that so many of their parents are not able to help them because they have very limited knowledge themselves.

The older adults that we encounter today were willing to believe in and commit to a religion on the basis of their grandmother's faith. They knew that if grandmother said it, it had to be true. If grandmother believed in God and witnessed to how he had always provided for her and her family and had "made a way out of no way," then it had to be true. If grandmother said that Jesus was the Son of God, had died to save her from her sins, and would come again for her and take her to her heavenly home, then it had to be true.

But that unquestioning acceptance of grandmother's faith is not good enough for the young people of the computer age. They want the facts, the data; they want proof. It becomes our responsibility as disciples of Christ to so commit our lives that we are in a position to help others make the same kind of commitment. We are charged with the responsibility of helping to make disciples.

Before we can commit ourselves to the Father and respond to our charge, we must find out who the Father is. The words of Paul to Timothy come immediately to mind: "Study to shew thyself approved unto God, a workman that needeth not to be ashamed, rightly dividing the word of truth" (2 Timothy 2:15 KJV). We must study God's word if we are to know him well enough to commit ourselves to him. I would not claim membership in a religion about which I knew nothing. I would not make a commitment to a God, pledge my life to him, feel bound to him, and place my trust in him if I did not have a personal relationship with him.

The Bible is the living book that introduces us to the experiences of others with the same God to whom we seek to make a commitment. In effect, the Bible becomes the source of the data that today's young people need. It was knowledge of the Bible that helped to crystallize their great-grandmother's faith.

As we read about the faith of those who lived in biblical times, we come to realize that as God delivered Daniel from the lions' den, so will he deliver us from the lions that we meet every day. We know that prayer was Daniel's weapon, and many times that same weapon has worked for me. As prayer closed the mouths of the lions in the den with Daniel, so has it closed the mouths of the lions who have harassed me in the workplace. Sometimes we are too happy, too well-dressed, or advancing too rapidly, and our co-worker lions attack us. Whenever these lions attacked me, I would smile and say, "I'll pray for you." You would have thought that I had promised to heap coals of fire on them, for after my promise of prayer, they kept their distance. They did not know the God I knew, and they were afraid that the stories they had heard about his power might really be true. I have been in the den of lions, and they have harmed me not. As this becomes my testimony, it serves to strengthen me. Prayer can also strengthen you.

Learning to Pray

In order to effectively use your prayer weapon, you must learn how to pray. In response to the disciples' request to teach them to pray, Jesus taught the Lord's Prayer (Matthew 6:7-13). While we need to follow the example of that prayer, we must also learn to say our own prayers. God hears the sincere and fervent prayers of saints and sinners alike. We cultivate a prayer life by praying with regularity and consistency. The

Jews pray three times a day, the Muslims five times a day, but the so-called Christians may not pray at all during the day. If we would learn to be his disciples, then we will be faithful in prayer. We just have to call on him, and he will answer. We ought to feel as though we have worried God too much, as though he is saying, "Oh, no. Not you again!" As his disciples, we call on God so much that we are never in doubt as to whether or not he recognizes our voice. God knows who we are because we have not made ourselves strangers to him. We have developed a personal relationship with him. He has become our Father.

As you seek to develop your relationship with God through prayer, consider these elements:

1. Every prayer you pray ought to include some praise, love, and admiration for God. Give him praise, for he is worthy! There is a gospel song that expresses this element so well. Its words are, "I can't miss a day praising his name. / I just can't forget from whence I came." The fact that we are yet alive bears witness to our having come from somewhere. Don't miss a day praising his name. To paraphrase the Negro spiritual, "If you don't praise him, the rocks will cry out; don't let the rocks cry in your place."

2. Then include some expressions of thanksgiving to the great God who has blessed you with life and health and strength. Consider all that he has done for you; isn't he worthy?

3. The next portion of your prayer should be devoted to confession. Remember the prayer of the sinner that was heard above all others, "God, be merciful to me, a sinner." (Luke 18:13*b*) We can all admit our sinfulness to God; after all, it is no surprise to him; he is already aware of everything we do. We just need to confess; confession is good for the soul. By confessing our sins we are reminded that none is good except God, and as we commit to him, we are striving to be more like him. And as his children, there ought to be some family resemblance.

4. The last part of our prayer is the part that so many of us begin with—the supplication, the requests. Always begin with requests for others first and for yourself last. What is it that you really want God to do for others and for you? What is it that you want God to help you do? Be selective; don't ask God to do everything for you; you can do some things for yourself. You have the power within you to do so much more for yourself than you can imagine. Where your knowl-

edge and power end, God's begins. So, all you need is the assurance of God's presence, and you have that. He promised never to leave you, and he never will.

In addition to the [...] you pray every-day at a designate[...] ou wake up in the morning or ret[...] learn to lift balloons of prayer up to [...] anytime during the day. Just a simple "Thank you," "Praise him," "Halleluia," or "Glory to God" will do. I like to think of these prayer expressions as balloons, for they take off and keep climbing, and that is what we want our prayers to do. If you release enough balloons during the day, you are assured that one is always out there working for you. God hears them, sees them, and knows that you have sent them and have your mind stayed on him.

Wouldn't you bless a child who was that faithful? Jesus said: "Is there anyone among you who, if your child asks for bread, will give a stone? Or if the child asks for a fish, will give a snake? If you then, who are evil, know how to give good gifts to your children, how much more will your Father in heaven give good things to those who ask him!" (Matthew 7:9-11). Think about it!

Follow a pattern like this as you cultivate

your prayer life. Include regularly scheduled prayer times, periodically release balloons of prayer, and constantly renew your commitment to the importance of prayer in your life. Once your commitment to prayer has become real, witness to others by volunteering to pray for them. Haven't you ever felt blessed when one of the saints of the church has told you that he or she was praying for you? I know that I have, and we can also become like one of those saints, witnessing to others. Once you know for a fact that prayer changes things, tell others. If you have experienced the power of prayer in your life, tell others. Witnessing is part of your commitment to the Father. It is a way of recruiting disciples.

Studying the Scriptures

Of course we will find out more about God as we experience communion with him through prayer, but the best way to discover who he is is through studying the scriptures. We meet the characters of the history of our faith in the Old Testament, and we learn the Good News in the New Testament. Any faith that claims to be Christian is based on the Bible, and the Bible is our book. We will never be able to commit to the Father if we do not know the Book. Let me suggest some ways that we can learn the contents of the Book.

1. The first way is to read the Book. By reading I mean to set aside a specific time each day to read the Word. Be faithful to the pattern you establish, and you will miss it if you break that pattern. I like to read when I first get up in the morning. I want the first thing I read to be God's Word. It gives me strength to face the day, and it is amazing how many times the words I have read come back to me during the day with new meaning. It is simply the voice of God speaking to me on my daily journey.

2. Purchase a study Bible with commentary and interpretations that will help to make the Scriptures meaningful to you. Just reading without understanding will not benefit you; you must digest what you read. Take the time to read the commentary as well as the Scriptures.

3. Set your own pace. Read the same chapter or verse as many times or days as necessary. Stay with it until you receive a blessing. Jacob wrestled with the angel and would not let go until he received a blessing. Wrestle with the Word, and do not let it go until you receive your blessing. I started reading the Bible every day at the age of twelve. I read a chapter a day and often had to reread them.

It took several years to read the entire Bible. I'm still reading every day and have read several different translations, and I'm still receiving a blessing.

4. If possible, join a Bible study class. Many religions have the requirement that prospective members attend a class to learn the beliefs and Scriptures, but many Christians claim salvation by the Blood and never bother to read the Book. Salvation is by the blood of Jesus, but we must also know and appreciate the Book. After all the Book tells us about the Blood. Most churches have Bible study classes and Sunday school classes that concentrate on Bible study. As you seek to commit to the Father, invest in the time to attend one of these classes, and be faithful in doing your homework.

5. Purchase and study videotapes, audiotapes, and records that provide Bible lessons. Here again, you can work at your own pace and replay the tapes or records as many times as you would like. Although many people like to study alone with these tools, I feel that there is much to be gained by viewing or listening with others. Sharing in a discussion often reveals insights that had been hidden. The Scriptures tell us in the words

of Jesus, "For where two or three are gathered in my name, I am there among them"
(Matthew 18:20). So, if there is no formal
Bible class organized in your vicinity, you
could form one by using the videotapes as
your instructor and following the plans and
questions outlined for discussion.

6. Spend time in meditation by reading,
studying, and committing Bible verses to
memory. We must hide the Word of God in
our hearts so that no one can take it away
from us. There will be times that you will
need the comfort of God's word, but the
only verses you know are, "Jesus wept" and
"The Lord is my Shepherd, I shall not
want." After those, many of us are lost.
Commit the Word to memory and it will
always be with you. I know that many of us
do not have the kind of memory that some
have. I know a man who can recite entire
books and chapters from the Bible without
ever looking at a single written word. It is a
marvelous gift, and whenever he needs the
comfort of God's word, it is hidden in his
heart. Maybe we cannot learn whole chapters, but we can learn several verses. Those
verses will magically appear just when we
need them most. It will be the voice of God

> speaking to us and reminding us of our being
> bound to him.

Getting to Know Jesus

As we journey on in our task of commitment
to the Father, let me refer you to Jesus, my Savior.
Jesus came to earth to reveal God more clearly to
us. "The Word became flesh and lived among us."
(John 1:14) Jesus is the Living Word. He made the
Word real to us through his life and death. We can
study his life and live the Word. Jesus is God with
us, so when we call on our Savior, Jesus Christ
the Son of God, we are calling on the Father.
Committing to Jesus and striving to live according to his example is committing to the Father.
Jesus is coexistent and coeternal with God, the
two of them form the Father and Son part of the
Trinity. For the Christian, "Thank you, Jesus" is
the same as "Thank you, God."

This Jesus, then, is someone that we who
would commit to the Father must get to know.
We must learn all that we can about his life and
ministry. In addition to the Bible study, we need
to read the history. We need to know that Jesus
was a real, flesh-and-blood person who lived and
died and was, during his lifetime, not very well
known outside the Roman Empire. We need to

know that his ministry was characterized by teaching, preaching, and healing. We need to know that he charged us to repent and believe the Good News. He expected his followers to love God and one another; he wanted his disciples to be different from others in the world, and he expected their light to shine so that others would see their good works and glorify their Father in heaven (Matthew 5:16).

Jesus has demonstrated real commitment. He gave his life in trust to his Father. He knew his Father was holding the rope, and he held on, even unto death on the cross. Real commitment was giving his life for the salvation of all. Our commitment is not that complete, for Jesus paid it all. Our task is to live the life he described in the Word.

I heard Ruth Graham, the wife of evangelist Billy Graham, talk about the blessing of committing to the Father. She said that she had always told her children, "You can call home, person-to-person and collect, anytime you want." She continued by saying, "That's what God allows and he has paid the price." Through his Son, Jesus, God paid the price and showed us how, through prayer, to call home anytime, person-to-person and collect. It's worth committing to a parent like that!

A Community of Believers

We've discussed prayer, meditation, and Bible study as means of getting to know the Father to whom we would make a commitment. But we must also affiliate with other believers. We must join a church. We need the fellowship of believers in order to witness to and grow in our faith. We are not on this life's journey by ourselves. The community of the called out and set apart faithful will sustain us through life's trials. The testimonies of believers will make the biblical stories relevant to daily life. The sermons, hymns, scriptures, creeds, and prayers will provide sustenance for the week.

We do so need a viable church experience on a steady basis that if your church is not providing that, find a new church, but don't stop going. Your need is too great and your commitment to the Father must be too complete for you to try to do it alone. There are enough Christians in your community for you to find your needs answered where you are. God may even be calling you to be the leader of his new community of faith.

Your community of faithful believers will help you as you face life's challenges. The list of challenges is endless, but consider these:

1. When you are being considered for a promotion, ask the church to pray for you.

2. When there is illness or death in your

family, ask the church to be your companion as you visit the hospital or the funeral home.

3. When employees are losing their jobs in your department, ask the church to join in prayer with you and for your job.

4. When your son or daughter is tempted by drugs, call on your Christian community.

God intends for us as Christians to be a supportive community. The church by definition is a supportive community. This is part of our commitment to him.

Our commitment to the Father gives us what we need to live moral and productive lives. When we see those around us committing crimes of violence, we know that they are not committed to the Father. When we encounter those who seek to limit us, we know that they are not committed to the Father. When we observe selfish and deceitful acts, we know that those committing them are not committed to the Father. Those who execute and perpetrate such acts have nothing to sustain them. The love of God does not enfold them because they have not sought it. They don't know who is holding the rope, and they have not been instructed to reach beyond the break and hold on.

We reach beyond the limitations in our life by developing our sense of self-esteem. Our Father helps us in this task because he has demonstrated to us how much we are really worth. He gave his Son for us. He has loved us unconditionally, and he never forsakes us. He has promised us the power to move mountains if we have faith and do not doubt, and he has guaranteed our salvation. If we commit to the Father, we certainly have self-esteem.

We reach beyond the limitations in our life by becoming successful. We must define our success and claim it. Only the Father can guarantee our satisfaction with our attainment in life, for if we seek first his kingdom, all else will be granted. However we define success, our Father has promised it to those who are committed to him.

We reach beyond the limitations in our life by finding sustenance in our unwavering commitment to the Father. He has given us the power to do anything we want. We can reach beyond the break. We can hold on. Praise God!